How Can I Be Healthy?

Exercise

Sarah Ridley

W

FRANKLIN WATTS

LONDON•SYDNEY

This edition 2010 by Franklin Watts
338 Euston Road, London NW1 3BH

Franklin Watts Australia
Level 17 / 207 Kent Street
Sydney, NSW 2000

Series editor: Melanie Palmer
Designed by: Pewter Design Associates
Series design: Peter Scoulding

How Can I Be Healthy? Exercise is a reduced text version of
The original text was by Beverely Goodger.

ISBN 978 0 7496 9590 3

Illustration: Michael Courtney, Mike Saunders, Guy Smith, Roger Stewart
Picture researcher: Sophie Hartley
Series consultant: Wendy Anthony, Health Education Unit, Education Service, Birmingham City Council
Picture credits: Action Images: 27. Samuel Ashfield/Science Photo Library: 5. © Bettmann/Corbis: 9.
Photo from www.JohnBirdsall.co.uk: 8. © J. de Bounevialle/Photofusion: 13t. © Jacky
Chapman/Photofusion: 24. Dr Ray Clark & Mervyn Goff/Science Photo Library: 32. Digital
Vision/Robert Harding: 35. Chad Ehlers/Alamy: 28. Chris Fairclough: 12, 13b, 14, 17, 29, 39. David
Gregs/Alamy: 10. Gusto/Science Photo Library: 31t. ImageState/Alamy: 11. © David Katzenberger/Corbis:
38. © Ute Klaphake/Photofusion: 4, 40, 45. © Julie Lemberger/Corbis: 18. © Ulrike Preuss/Photofusion:
33. © Roger Ressmeyer/Corbis: 37. Françoise Sauze/Science Photo Library: 19t. Thinkstock/Alamy: 23. ©
Frank Trapper/Corbis: 25. © E.H. Wallop/Corbis: 41. © Franklin Watts Publishers: 21, 30, 31b. ©
Catherine Wessel/Corbis: 19b.

The Publisher would like to thank the Brunswick Club for Young People, Fulham, London for their help
with this book. Thanks to our models, including Stevie Waite.

A CIP catalogue record for this book is available from the British Library.

Printed in Malaysia

Franklin Watts is a division of Hachette Children's Books, an Hachette UK company.
www.hachette.co.uk

Contents

Exercise and your body   8

Why should we exercise?   10

Stamina   12

The heart   14

The lungs   16

Suppleness   18

Joints   20

Muscles   22

Strength   24

The immune system   26

Mood   28

A balanced diet   30

Exercise and food   32

Releasing energy   34

Face the facts   36

Exercise every day   38

How to exercise   40

Glossary   42

Further information   43

Index   44

Exercise and your body

To stay healthy, you need to eat well and exercise regularly. This is especially important for children and young people as their bodies are still developing. If you are fit, you are much more likely to fight off illness and enjoy life to the full.

This girl is testing her strength and her courage on a climbing wall.

Regular exercise
Children between the ages of 5 and 18 should do something active for at least an hour a day.

There are many ways to do this: Choose from running, walking, skipping, cycling, tennis, football, swimming – and plenty more!

Get moving

Some people enjoy organised sport and join a team. But everyone can become more active just by walking to school or to the shops, using the stairs instead of the lift, or dancing to music at home.

Past and present

In the past, children were more active. They played outside, rode their bikes and walked to school. There were not many televisions or any computers. Today some children are becoming unhealthy because they take so little exercise.

Your view

Why do you think some people use the car, even for short journeys? What could be done to encourage them to walk or cycle instead?

It's your life

How could you become more active? Could you walk or cycle to school? Do you enjoy dancing? What school sports club would you like to join?

Children play roller-hockey in a 1930s street in the USA. Children spent much more time outside in the past.

Why should we exercise?

Exercise is good for our health. It improves our fitness in three different ways. It gives us more stamina, suppleness and strength. Exercise also helps us to relax and sleep well.

Stamina

People with good stamina can keep going for a long time. Activities such as gentle jogging, fast walking, swimming and cycling help to build up stamina. They make the heart and lungs work well so that the body does not get tired easily.

▼ Gymnastics helps to develop suppleness, strength and balance.

Suppleness

Suppleness, or flexibility, allows the body to bend and move easily. It improves the way we stand and helps to prevent injuries.

It's your life

Is one form of exercise enough? Each activity has a different effect on the body. Look at the chart (right) to find out more about stamina, suppleness and strength.

"I love running. It makes me feel happy and full of energy. I love being outside."

Eliza, aged 10

Stamina, suppleness and strength

Exercise	Stamina	Suppleness	Strength
Badminton	good effects	very good effects	good effects
Baseball	good effects	little effect	good effects
Basketball	very good effects	good effects	very good effects
Cycling	excellent effects	good effects	very good effects
Dancing (fast)	very good effects	excellent effects	good effects
Football	good effects	good effects	good effects
Gymnastics	good effects	excellent effects	very good effects
Jogging	excellent effects	good effects	good effects
Judo	good effects	very good effects	good effects
Rollerblading	very good effects	little effect	good effects
Skipping (fast)	excellent effects	little effect	good effects
Swimming	excellent effects	excellent effects	excellent effects
Tennis	good effects	very good effects	good effects
Walking	good effects	little effect	little effect

Key:

X	:‑)	:‑D	:‑D (filled)
little effect	good effects	very good effects	excellent effects

▲ Playing football builds strength and is fun!

Strength

If the body's muscles and bones are strong, it allows the person to run, climb and be active. Strong muscles also protect the body from injury.

Stamina

Stamina allows someone to exercise for longer without getting tired. People can build up stamina by exercising the heart and the lungs. Here are two types of stamina-building exercise:

Steady exercise

Some forms of exercise are carried out at a steady pace. Walking, skipping, swimming and cycling all fall into this group. To build stamina you need to get slightly out of breath and feel warm when carrying out exercise.

Skipping improves stamina.

Your view

Why do you think people often choose not to do any exercise, even though they know it will make them fit?

Intense exercise

Your body also needs short bursts of hard exercise to build stamina. Sprinting is a good example. Expect to get out of breath and warm or hot with this type of exercise.

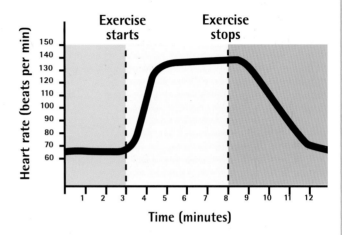

Athletes have very fast recovery times after exercise.

Changes in pulse rate with exercise

Heart rate (beats per min)

Exercise starts — Exercise stops

150 140 130 120 110 100 90 80 70 60

1 2 3 4 5 6 7 8 9 10 11 12

Time (minutes)

Feel the pulse

Your pulse rate is one way to measure how fit you are. Feel your wrist pulse: it is under the skin, just below the thumb joint. Count the number of pulse beats in 60 seconds to give your resting pulse. Now carry out a minute of energetic exercise. Measure your pulse

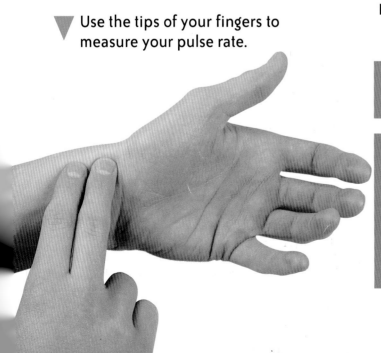

Use the tips of your fingers to measure your pulse rate.

rate again. It will be higher. How long does it take to return to the first measurement? The amount of time it takes for your pulse rate to return to its resting rate is called the recovery time. The faster your recovery time, the fitter you are.

My experience

"I think it is easier for boys to keep fit than girls. I like running around at lunchtime but my friends just want to stand and chat."

Kirstie, aged 12

The heart

The heart pumps blood around the body. The blood travels along blood vessels to all the cells of the body, carrying food and oxygen.

Heartbeat

The human heart beats about 70 times a minute without stopping. That's over 100,000 times a day. It is a muscle that never rests, pushing blood out of the heart and into the bloodstream with every beat.

Low-oxygen blood enters the heart from the upper body

Blood filled with oxygen is pumped into the bloodstream

low-oxygen blood is pumped out to the lungs, where the blood absorbs oxygen again

Blood filled with oxygen enters the heart from the lungs

Oxygen-poor blood enters the heart from the lower body

▲ When the heart beats, it squeezes blood out of the heart. More blood rushes in and it all happens again.

► This boy is showing the position and size of his heart inside his body.

Your experience

▶ "I swim at a club twice a week. Sometimes we work on our strokes but often we build up our stamina by swimming up and down the pool for the whole time. I used to get really tired but now I find it much easier."
Ben, aged 11

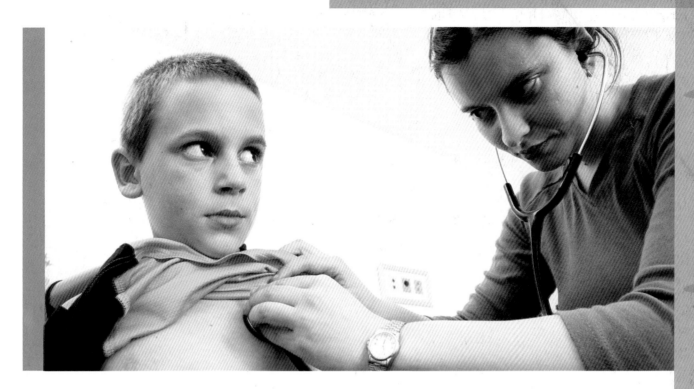

Doctors use a stethoscope to listen to their patients' heartbeat.

Exercise your heart

Like all muscles, the heart muscle grows stronger through exercise. When you exercise, you can feel your heart pumping more quickly. This is good for the heart as it helps to keep it in good shape for a lifetime. Stamina-building exercise is especially good for the heart.

Stay healthy

The fat in some types of food can build up on the inside of the blood vessels. This can lead to heart disease and even death.

However, when the heart pumps more strongly after exercise, it helps to prevent the build-up of this fat on the walls of the blood vessels (see pages 36–37).

It's your life

Are you looking after your heart? Children who don't take much exercise are much more likely to gain weight and are more likely to develop heart disease and other illnesses in later life.

The lungs

Like the heart, the lungs never stop working. They are the body's breathing machine, providing the body's cells with the oxygen they need to keep working.

The lungs and exercise

Stamina-building exercise makes the body breathe faster and harder than it does when at rest. This strengthens the diaphragm and other muscles which control our breathing movements.

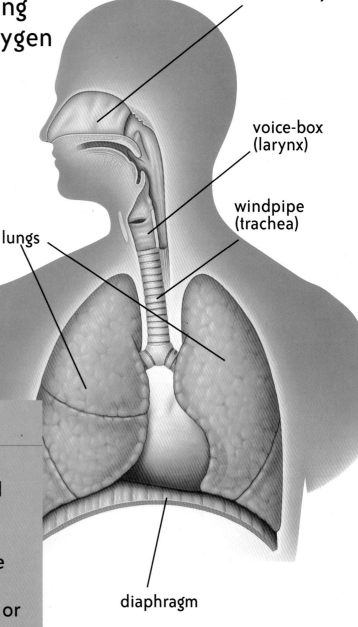

nasal cavity

voice-box (larynx)

windpipe (trachea)

lungs

diaphragm

▲ Air enters through the nose and mouth and passes to the lungs. There, the oxygen in the air is absorbed into the bloodstream.

Your decision

Do you suffer from asthma? Some people with asthma find that exercise can bring on an attack. However, everyone should take exercise. Take care to build up the exercise gradually and ask your doctor or asthma nurse for help if you have problems. Paula Radcliffe, the marathon runner, has learnt to manage her asthma.

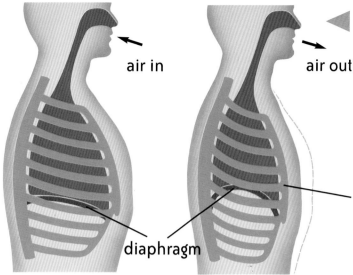

air in

air out

◁ Each breath contains about half a litre of air.

Muscles are attached to the ribs. They make them move in and out when we breathe.

diaphragm

This diagram shows the body breathing in air.

This diagram shows the body breathing out air.

Breathing in and out

When we breathe in, the diaphragm flattens and muscles pull the rib cage upwards. This increases the space in the chest so that the lungs can expand, sucking in air from the windpipe that joins up to the nose and the mouth.

When we breathe out, the diaphragm pushes up and the muscles pull the rib cage down and in. This pushes air out of the lungs and out of the body.

It's your life

Smoking is bad for your lungs. Once people have started smoking it can be difficult to stop. Gradually smokers may find that they become breathless, even after walking up the stairs. Young people who smoke make their heart and lungs work very hard when they exercise. They will tire more quickly and become more breathless than non-smokers.

Even young smokers can suffer from coughs caused by cigarettes. ▶

Suppleness

Suppleness means how flexible your body is – how easily you can bend and stretch. If you are supple, you will be able to make a wide range of movements using your muscles and joints.

Your experience

"Last term my class were involved in a dance workshop. It was amazing – the dancers were so flexible and fit. I really enjoyed the workshops that followed and now I belong to a dance group."

Jo, aged 13

Ballet dancers are superb athletes. Their ballet training develops their suppleness, stamina and strength so that they can dance beautifully.

It's your life

Most children are supple, so they can bend easily. How will you make sure you stay bendy in later life?

Doing yoga can maintain suppleness. ▶

Achieving suppleness

Suppleness is developed through gentle stretching. Stretching exercises should be part of your warm up and warm down routine when you take part in sport or other activities (see pages 40-41). Activities such as yoga, swimming, dancing and gymnastics all develop suppleness.

How supple are you?

Try this test. Sit on the floor with your legs in front of you. If you can reach beyond your toes you are very supple. If you can only reach your ankles you need to work on your suppleness.

▼ It is important for footballers to be supple to prevent injuries and to allow them to dodge and run after the ball.

Joints

A place where two bones meet is called a joint. Some joints, like those in the skull, don't move, and are called fixed joints. Most joints in the body can move about, and play a part in making us flexible.

shoulder: ball and socket joint

elbow: hinge joint

▲ Keeping joints supple helps us to move freely.

Ligaments and tendons

Bones are held together at the joints by tough, elastic bands, called ligaments. Skeletal muscles are attached to the bones that they pull on by tough cords or strings, called tendons.

By keeping the muscles supple, or bendy, you can help to take care of your joints. If you are not very supple, or if you suddenly bend a joint in the wrong direction, the tendons, ligaments or muscles can be damaged.

A diagram showing the knee joint. It is a hinge joint because it only allows movement backwards and forwards. ▶

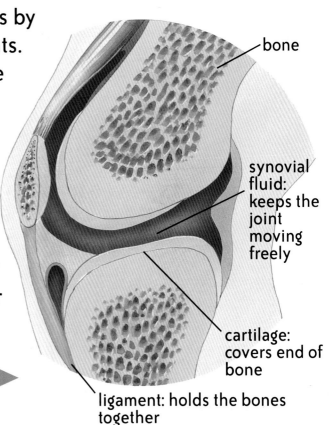

bone

synovial fluid: keeps the joint moving freely

cartilage: covers end of bone

ligament: holds the bones together

Your experience

"Last year I sprained my ankle twice when playing tennis. My doctor gave me a set of exercises to improve my flexibility and balance to help stop me from doing it again."

Chloe, aged 12

Looking after your joints

Flexible muscles and smoothly working joints make sure that all the parts of your body are held in the right place. Regular exercise helps to keep joints flexible and keeps the muscles strong, allowing the body to stay stronger for longer into old age.

It's your life

Try to eat foods containing calcium every day. Calcium is present in dairy foods such as milk, cheese, butter and yoghurt. It is also found in dark green vegetables, some pulses and certain seeds, such as sunflower seeds. Calcium helps you to develop strong bones and joints, to last into old age.

Eating foods that contain calcium helps to build strong bones and joints.

▼ Dairy foods, such as cheese, milk, butter and yoghurt, provide the calcium needed by the body.

Muscles

The body contains 640 skeletal muscles. These muscles pull on the bones of the skeleton to make the body move and to hold it upright.

Pull, not push

Skeletal muscles can only contract (shorten) and relax. They work in pairs to move parts of the body. When one arm muscle contracts, it pulls the arm up. To straighten the arm again, another muscle contracts, to pull it back again, while the first muscle relaxes.

The structure of skeletal muscle

Skeletal muscles are made of long, rod-shaped cells called muscle fibres, and can be up to 30 cm long. Each muscle fibre is made of thousands of thinner strands.

The skeletal muscles at the front of the body.

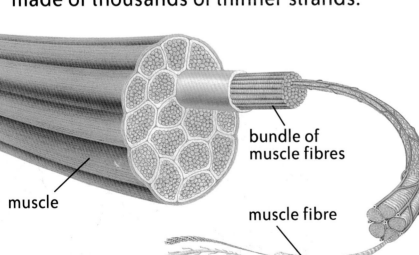

muscle

bundle of muscle fibres

muscle fibre

Running through each skeletal muscle are hundreds of thousands of long, thin muscle fibres.

biceps muscle
contracts

▼ Muscles work in pairs to move
bones at a joint. Here, the
biceps muscle moves the
arm up (left), while the
triceps muscle pulls it
straight again (right).

biceps muscle
relaxes

triceps
muscle
contracts

triceps muscle
relaxes

Muscles
and exercise

Exercise improves
the muscles' strength:
it makes the body
stronger, so we are able
to do more things.

This
happens
especially
when we do
exercises that make
our muscles work
hard. When muscles
recover from this stress
their fibres get bigger, making
them stronger and more powerful.

◄ Some people use weight exercise to
increase the size of their muscles
because they like the way this makes
their body look.

Your view

▶ Sometimes athletes take illegal
drugs to build up their muscles.
What do you think makes these
athletes risk their careers?

Strength

A strong body will allow you to throw yourself into exercise. When we talk about strength, we are referring to how strong our muscles are. The stronger our muscles are, the better they will perform in everyday tasks or in sport.

Swimming builds muscle strength.

▼

Use your muscles

The more we use our muscles, the healthier and stronger they become. When we use a muscle to lift, push or pull things, it makes that muscle get larger. If we do not use a muscle, it grows weak.

Your experience

"When I broke my arm, it was in a plaster cast for six weeks. When they took the plaster cast off, my arm looked really thin, and felt very weak. It took a while before the muscles built up again."

Jack, aged 13

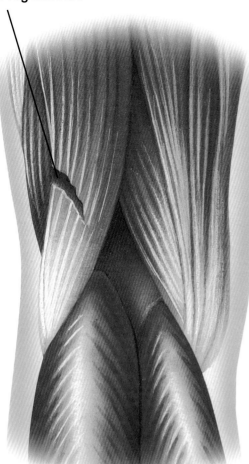

torn leg muscle

Strong muscles

Strong muscles pull hard on the bones to produce strong movements. This helps to strengthen the bones, making them less likely to break. Strong muscles also give good support to the joints, reducing the risk of injury.

Muscle problems

Muscles need rest after taking a lot of exercise. This recovery period gives them time to build up and reduces the risk of injury.

◄ Sudden movements can make a muscle tear. The muscle has to be rested so that it can heal.

Your view

Fit people have a good body shape. While most people agree that strong muscles are important for health and fitness, is there too much pressure on people to have the perfect body?

When TV programmes focus on slim, beautiful people, it can make many viewers feel unhappy with their appearance. But men and women who play sports often have a more positive view of themselves and are affected less by what's on the television. ▶

The immune system

The body's immune system fights off illness and kills germs. Research suggests that moderate exercise helps the immune system to work well.

When to exercise

Recent research has shown that our immune system is at its weakest early in the morning. This means that we are most at risk of catching germs at this time. The best time to take serious exercise may be around 6 pm – the time of day when the immune system is at its peak. For most people, however, light exercise at any time of day helps our immune system to work well.

Exercise and illness

Although exercise is good for the body, it is best not to take exercise if you have a heavy cold or a fever. Resting for a day or two will give the immune system a chance to fight the infection. Research shows that it is safe to exercise, if you feel like it, if you only have a light cold and no fever.

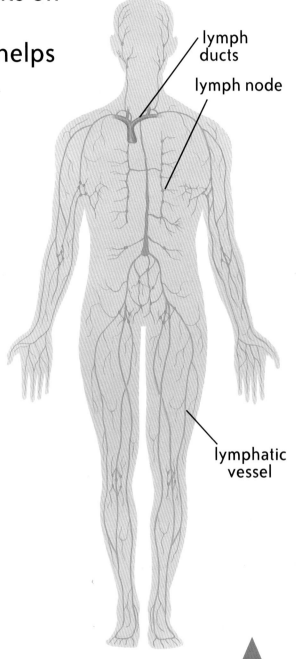

lymph ducts

lymph node

lymphatic vessel

The lymphatic system, shown in green, reaches all parts of the body. It plays a vital role in fighting infection. When muscles squeeze and relax they help move the liquids in the lymphatic system around the body.

It's your life

Should you exercise when you are ill? It's sometimes best to rest, and not exercise, when we are feeling unwell. It will depend how ill you feel. How will you decide?

Risk of infection compared with amount of training

Risk of infection

Increased

Normal

Decreased

Sedentary   Moderate   Very high

Amount of exercise

Too much exercise?

Some scientists have carried out research which showed that too much exercise can lower the immune system. This research showed that marathon runners were more likely to develop a cold after a marathon.

Marathon running is very tiring. Marathon runners have to take care not to fall ill after a marathon.

Your experience

"Since I joined the running club, I feel so much healthier. I don't know whether it stops me getting ill but I feel so much fitter and stronger than I did before."

Mike, aged 14

Mood

Exercise can make us feel good. It helps to improve concentration and co-ordination, and it can make us feel better about ourselves. It can also help us to make friends.

It can be great fun to meet people who enjoy playing the same sport as you.

Endorphins

Some forms of exercise make you feel happy because they cause the brain to release chemicals called endorphins. These send feel-good messages around the body.

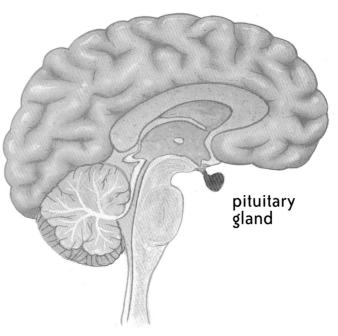

pituitary gland

▶ The pituitary gland in the brain releases endorphins.

Exercise addicts

Some people seem to become addicted to exercise and the feelings of happiness they experience from the release of endorphins. Exercise addicts can damage their bodies because they exercise even when they are ill, injured or need a meal.

Winning and losing

When you win a race or a match, you can feel on top of the world. But if you lose, it can make you feel unhappy. Learning to deal with the ups and the downs of competitive sport is all part of being an athlete.

Your experience

"My sister wants to be very slim. She started off exercising three times a week, but now she goes to the gym, plays tennis or something every day. She is hardly ever in and she neglects her friends and family. It makes me feel sad that we never spend time together any more."

Chloe, aged 10

When people eat chocolate, it acts on the pituitary gland, causing it to release endorphins.

It's your life

Both eating chocolate and taking exercise can make you feel happy, but too much chocolate can also make you put on weight! So why not get that happy feeling by being outside and being active. If you take up a sport and find that you are really good at it, this can also make you feel good about yourself.

A balanced diet

Exercise alone cannot make you fit. You also need to eat all the right types of food to make your body work as well as possible.

The pyramid shows the amounts of each food group, or nutrient, you should try to eat each day. You need far more carbohydrates than fats in your diet.

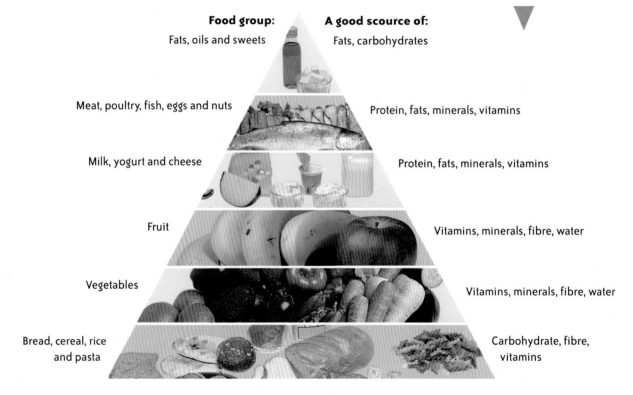

Food group: | **A good scource of:**

Fats, oils and sweets — Fats, carbohydrates

Meat, poultry, fish, eggs and nuts — Protein, fats, minerals, vitamins

Milk, yogurt and cheese — Protein, fats, minerals, vitamins

Fruit — Vitamins, minerals, fibre, water

Vegetables — Vitamins, minerals, fibre, water

Bread, cereal, rice and pasta — Carbohydrate, fibre, vitamins

Your view

We learn so much about what is good for us to eat and what makes a balanced diet. Why do you think so many people ignore the advice? What could be done to help them eat more healthily?

Too much or too little

To stay healthy, the body needs the right amounts of the right foods. Eat too little and the body may stop working properly. Eat too much and the body will put down fat. A balanced diet gives the body all it needs.

Food groups

The food we eat can be divided into four main food groups: Carbohydrates provide the body with its energy needs.

What is in your favourite snack?

	Ready salted crisps (100g)	Milk chocolate (100g)	Apple (100g)
Carbohydrate	50.7g	57.1g	11.8g
Protein	6.6g	7.8g	0.4g
Fat	35.1g	29.9g	0.1g

Proteins are used to help the body grow and repair itself. Fats are also used for energy and help to keep the body warm. Vitamins and minerals help the body to work well and fight off disease.

Crisps are a popular snack but are high in fat. They are not a good choice after taking exercise. ▶

It's your life

Famous footballers and other athletes follow lots of advice about what to eat when they are training, or before a big event. Do you try to follow advice about how to eat well?

Drink water!

Our bodies need between six and eight glasses of water each day to work well. When we exercise, our bodies sweat more because sweating helps to cool down our bodies. We must replace this lost water, and this will mean drinking extra water, although many foods contain water as well.

Exercise and food

Without food, the cells of the body will stop working. The energy from food is used by the body to grow and repair itself, as well as to move about in everyday life.

Food for exercise

When you take exercise your body needs energy. Your body gets this energy from foods rich in carbohydrate, such as bread or pasta. If you are a bit overweight, the body will gradually use up some of the fat stored around your body to release energy.

Your experience

"After my swimming lesson, I'm starving. I could eat anything and everything! I try to take a healthy snack with me."

Megan, aged 8

When the body uses energy, heat is produced. In this special photo, called a thermograph, you can see which muscles are being used the most by a man on a bicycle. Their heat shows up as red or orange.

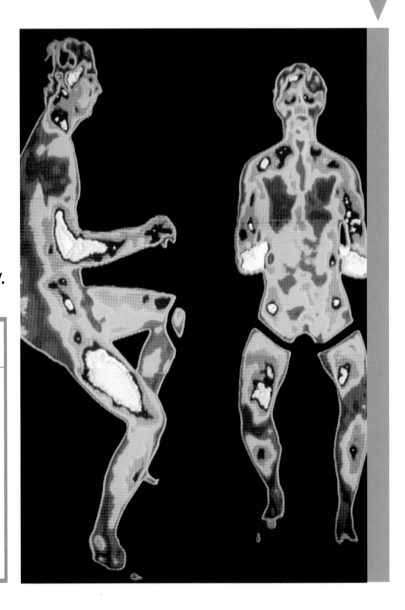

Timing meals

It puts a strain on the body if you exercise straight after eating a meal. Try to leave two or three hours between a meal and taking exercise. If you need a snack, try fruit or a cereal bar and eat a main meal later.

Everyone needs to eat different amounts of food, depending on how active they are. Teenage boys need to eat the most food as they are growing, they tend to be active and they have started to build up muscles.

Energy in food is usually measured in units called calories or kilocalories or sometimes joules. This chart shows the average number of calories that young people of different ages need each day.

Average calorie requirements for children and teenagers (kilocalories per day)

	Boys	Girls
7-10 years	1,970	1,740
11-14 years	2,220	1,845
15-18 years	2,755	2,110

Releasing energy

Have you ever wondered how the body releases energy from the food we eat?

Digestion

Food is broken down into tiny nutrients inside the stomach and intestines in a process called digestion. Nutrients are absorbed into the blood and carried around the body in blood vessels.

Cell respiration

The body is built from living cells. One type of nutrient, glucose, and oxygen pass into the cells from the blood circulating around the body. The mitochondria found inside each

Inside a mitochondrion, chemical reactions occur that release the energy stored in glucose. Carbon dioxide is a waste product that is breathed out by the lungs.

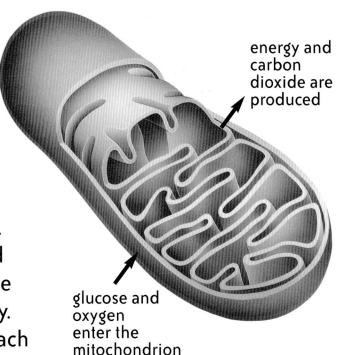

energy and carbon dioxide are produced

glucose and oxygen enter the mitochondrion

Did you know?

Teenage boys need to eat more food than teenage girls. This is because, on average, girls are smaller than boys but it is also because boys have more muscle cells. Muscle cells contain more mitochondria which use up the energy from food more quickly.

Your experience

"My legs feel wobbly after a race with my friends but they soon recover after I catch my breath."

Jason, aged 9

cell use oxygen to release energy from glucose. This is called cell respiration. The energy released by this is used by the cell and keeps it alive.

Some cells use more energy than others. Muscle cells use a lot of energy and have a lot of

mitochondria inside them to supply energy. During exercise, the heart beats much faster to supply the muscle cells with plenty of blood carrying oxygen and glucose for cell respiration to occur. Then the muscles have the energy to keep working.

After a sprint race, the sprinters have to pant (breathe fast and deeply) to get oxygen back into their lungs.

Face the facts

If people don't take care of their health, they risk developing diseases such as heart disease, cancer and diabetes.

Fats in the blood

The body breaks down the food we eat into nutrients, including fats. The blood carries oxygen and nutrients around the body. If someone eats a lot of fatty foods,

Fats can build up inside the arteries, narrowing the blood vessels and stopping the blood from flowing freely around the body.

blood flow

fatty substance in an artery

such as crisps and biscuits, fats can end up sticking to the walls of the blood vessels called arteries. If the arteries supplying the heart become narrow or blocked, a heart attack may occur. Exercise can help to keep the fat moving through the arteries and back to the liver, where the liver will deal with it.

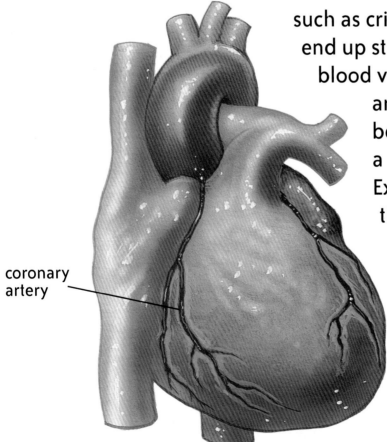

coronary artery

The heart muscle needs oxygen and food to keep it working properly. This is carried in the blood and reaches the heart through the coronary artery, left.

Energy balance

If someone eats more food than they need, they will gain weight. Doctors know that being overweight puts people at risk of developing many illnesses and health conditions. Exercise can help to keep a balance between the amount of energy that is eaten and the amount that is used every day.

▲ Obesity in children is increasing in many parts of the world.

Childhood obesity

Children who don't take regular exercise and who eat too much may become obese. Obese children are likely to become obese adults, increasing their risk of developing heart disease, diabetes, high blood pressure and cancer.

Your view

▶ Should the government do more to help people take more exercise? What ideas could you suggest that might encourage people to become more active?

Your experience

▶ "My grandfather had a mild heart attack two years ago. Now he eats more healthily."

Laura, aged 9

Exercise every day

We only need to exercise for 60 minutes out of the 1,440 minutes in a day! It really is worth finding the time to take exercise. You will feel better and stronger – and you will live longer!

Martial arts are one way of taking exercise and making friends at the same time.

It's your life

Do you exercise for at least 60 minutes a day? Perhaps you could meet friends at the park? Does your local pool offer free swimming sessions? See what you can do to get moving.

Get moving

Some people are in all the school sports teams. But even if you are not good at school sports, it doesn't mean you

Some fitness tips

1. If you can, walk to and from school each day, or to the local shops.

2. Try to be active during break and lunchtime at school – walk about, or join a club such as one for football, hockey or table tennis.

3. Try a new sport such as a martial art, dancing, volleyball or trampolining. Your local leisure centre may offer classes, or your school may run clubs.

4. Try some active jobs to help at home – gardening, vacuuming the carpets and cleaning the windows all use energy.

5. Eat fruit when you want a quick snack, or try a slice of bread (preferably brown). Ask your parents to buy less sweets and fatty foods.

6. Try to eat five portions of different fruit and vegetables each day and drink plenty of water.

Your experience

"Since I took up judo, I take much more exercise. It has also taught me how important it is to work at something if you want to improve – so my school work has improved as well!"

Jo, aged 12

▼ Fresh fruit make a great snack and can help keep you healthy so that you can enjoy taking exercise.

should give up on exercise. Walking, dancing and cycling are just as good for the body and are easy for everyone to do.

How to exercise

Avoid damaging your body by following the advice on this page. After exercise, you need to feel warm and slightly out of breath. And you need to take exercise every day to stay fit.

How to exercise

- If you have any medical conditions, such as asthma, get checked out by a doctor first.
- Choose the time and the place carefully – don't exercise after a heavy meal – and stay safe – avoid busy roads, uneven ground or lonely places.
- Warm up before exercising – this will prepare your muscles, heart and lungs for their work-out.
- Drink plenty of water before, during and after exercise.
- Warm down when you've finished – this will help to keep you supple, and will prevent stiffness from setting in the next day.
- Vary the exercises and enjoy it. Variety will also ensure that you exercise a range of muscles.
- Keep yourself and your kit clean. Sweating is a normal, healthy part of taking exercise, but keep healthy by washing yourself and your clothes.

Exercise should be fun!

Ways of warming up

Warm-up exercises should be done slowly and smoothly.

- Begin with some gentle exercise, such as jogging, to warm up muscles and to prepare the heart and lungs for action.

- Then do some gentle neck stretching exercises, circle the arms and finally do some side bends. These movements will help to loosen the muscles which move our joints in the neck, shoulders and back.

- Gently stretch all the leg muscles to avoid injury once you start working them hard.

Your experience

"I think I'm active for at least an hour each day. I walk to and from the bus stop, I play football with my friends at break time. We have two lessons of games or PE each week, and I do an after-school sport club once a week. I ride my bike, or go swimming at the weekend. Mind you, I do enjoy sitting still and playing a computer game!"

James, aged 12

It's your life

It is never too late to take up exercise. People who take up exercise in middle-age live longer than those that don't.

◀ This athlete is doing gentle leg stretches.

And finally...

Warming down is as important as warming up. A gentle jog could be followed by the stretching and bending exercises used to warm up.

Glossary

Addiction: a habit that is hard to stop.

Asthma: a health condition that can make it difficult to breathe.

Balanced diet: eating the right amounts of all the different nutrients.

Blood pressure: the pressure of blood pressing against the blood vessels as it flows around the body.

Blood vessels: the veins, arteries and capillaries that carry blood.

Calcium: a mineral needed by the body to build strong bones and teeth.

Calorie: a unit of energy. One kilocalorie(Kcal) = 4 kilojoules (KJ).

Carbohydrates: food group including bread, cereals, pasta, rice and potatoes and which supplies energy.

Cell: a tiny unit of living material.

Diabetes: a disease of the pancreas when the body doesn't produce enough, or any, insulin, to digest sugars in food.

Diaphragm: the muscle which makes the lungs expand and contract.

Endorphin: a chemical released in the brain which makes us feel happy.

Fats: nutrients that include oils, butter, cheese and fats in meat or fish.

Germs: very tiny things that can cause illness.

Glucose: a simple form of sugar

Heart disease: all diseases of the heart and of the blood vessels supplying the heart.

Immune system: the body system that fights off illness and kills germs.

Joints: place where two bones meet.

Ligaments: a tough, elastic band of body tissue that holds bones together.

Lungs: the body's breathing machine.

Minerals: nutrients, such as calcium, iron and potassium, that your body needs in small amounts.

Mitochondria: tiny structures inside body cells producing energy.

Nutrients: the parts of food used by the body for growth and energy.

Proteins: nutrients found in meat, fish, dairy products and pulses.

Pulse: each heartbeat is felt as a throb, or pulse, at certain points on the body.

Recovery time: the time it takes for the pulse to return to its resting rate.

Stamina: being able to carry on exercising for long periods of time.

Suppleness: being able to move and bend the body easily.

Tendons: a tough cord or string that attaches a muscle to a bone.

Vitamins: one of over 13 substances, including vitamins C and D, needed in small amounts in a person's diet.

Further information

UK
Bike for all
Information about cycling, safe routes and other cycle advice.
www.bikeforall.net/index.php

Change4Life
An NHS website packed with information about how to become more active. Also lots of ideas about swimming, cycling, walking and active play.
www.nhs.uk/change4life/Pages/Default.aspx

Eat well, be well
Food Standards Agency website that focuses on healthy eating. Gives advice on eating a good diet for sport.
www.eatwell.gov.uk/

Active places
Search for sports facilities close to where you live using this website funded by Sport England.
www.activeplaces.com/

AUSTRALIA
The Australian Sports Commission
This website also incorporates the Australian Institute of Sport. The websites are full of information about all aspects of sport, including advice about training and diet.
www.ausport.gov.au/

Children's Youth and Women's Health Service (South Australia)
Lots of information about how the body works.
www.cyh.com/Default.aspx?p=1

Note to parents and teachers: Every effort has been made by the Publishers to ensure that these websites are suitable for children, that they are of the highest educational value, and that they contain no inappropriate or offensive material. However, because of the nature of the Internet, it is impossible to guarantee that the contents of these sites will not be altered. We strongly advise that Internet access is supervised by a responsible adult.

Index

asthma 16, 40, 42
athletes 13, 18, 23, 29, 31, 41

balanced diet 30-33, 42
blood 14, 15, 16, 34, 35, 36, 42
blood pressure 37, 42
bones 11, 20, 21, 22, 23, 24, 25, 42
brain 28, 42
breathing 16-17, 34

calcium 21, 42
calories 33, 42
cancer 36, 37
carbohydrates 30, 31, 32, 35, 42
cell respiration 34-35
cells 14, 16, 32, 34, 35, 42
cycling 8, 9, 10, 11, 12, 32, 39

dancing 9, 11, 18, 19, 39
diabetes 36, 37, 42
diaphragm 16, 17, 42
digestion 34

endorphins 28, 29, 42
exercise addicts 29

fats 15, 30, 31, 32, 36, 42
football 8, 11, 19, 31, 41

germs 26, 42
glucose 34, 35
gymnastics 10, 11, 19

heart 10, 12, 14-15, 16, 17, 35, 36, 40, 41, 42
heart disease 15, 36, 37, 42

illness 8, 15, 26, 27, 29, 36, 37, 42
immune system 26-27, 42
injuries 10, 11, 19, 20, 21, 25, 29, 40, 41

joints 13, 18, 20-21, 23, 25, 41, 42

ligaments 20, 42
lungs 10, 12, 14, 16-17, 34, 35, 40, 41, 42
lymphatic system 26

marathon runners 16, 27
minerals 30, 42
mitochondria 34, 35, 42
mood 28-29
muscles 11, 14, 15, 16, 17, 18, 20, 21, 22-25, 26, 32, 33, 34, 35, 36, 40, 41, 42
muscle fibres 22, 23

nutrients 30 34, 36, 42

overweight 32, 37
oxygen 14, 16, 34, 35, 36

proteins 30, 31, 42
pulse 13, 15, 42

recovery time 13, 42
running 8, 10, 11, 12, 13, 16, 27, 35

skipping 8, 11, 12
smoking 17
stamina 10, 11, 12, 13, 14, 15, 16, 18, 42
strength 8, 10, 11, 18, 21, 23, 24-25
stretching exercises 19, 41
suppleness 10, 11, 18-19, 20, 21, 40, 42
swimming 8, 10, 11, 12, 14, 19, 24, 32, 38, 41

team sport 9, 38, 39
tendons 20, 42
tennis 8, 11, 21, 29

vitamins 30, 31, 42

walking 8, 9, 10, 11, 12, 39, 41
water 30, 31, 39, 40